MW00609944

THE DIVINE SONGS OF ZARATHUSHTRA

BY

D. J. IRANI

WITH AN INTRODUCTION
BY
RABINDRANATH TAGORE

LONDON: GEORGE ALLEN & UNWIN LTD.
RUSKIN HOUSE, 40 MUSEUM STREET, W.C. 1
NEW YORK: THE MACMILLAN COMPANY

First published in 1924

Printed in Great Britain by
UNWIN BROTHERS, LIMITED, LONDON AND WOKING

THE DIVINE SONGS OF ZARAṬHUSHTRA

INTRODUCTION

THE most important of all outstanding facts of Iranian history is the religious reform brought about by Zarathushtra. He was the first man we know who gave a definitely moral character and direction to religion, and at the same time preached the doctrine of monotheism, which offered an eternal foundation of reality to goodness as an ideal of perfection. All religions of the primitive type try to keep men bound with regulations of external observances. These, no doubt, have the hypnotic effect of vaguely suggesting a realm of right and wrong; but the dimness of their light produces phantasms leaving men to aberrations. Zarathushtra was the greatest of all the pioneer prophets who showed the path of freedom to men, the freedom of moral choice, the freedom from blind obedience to unmeaning injunctions, freedom from the multiplicity of shrines which draw our worship away from the single-minded chastity of devotion. To most of us it sounds like a truism to-day when we are told that the moral goodness of a deed comes from the goodness of intention. But it is a truth which once came to a man like a revelation of light in the darkness and has not yet reached all the obscure corners of humanity. There are men we still see around us who fearfully follow, hoping thereby to gain merit, the path of blind formalisms, which have no living moral source in the mind. This will make us understand the greatness of Zarathushtra. Though surrounded by believers in magical rites, he proclaimed in those dark days of unreason, that religion has its truth in its moral significance, not in external practices of imaginary value; that it is to uphold man in his life of good thoughts, good words and good deeds.

The outer expression of truth reaches its white light of simplicity through its inner realisation. True simplicity is the physiognomy of perfection. In the primitive stage of spiritual growth, when man is dimly aware of the mystery of the infinite in his life and the world, when he does not fully know the inward character of his relationship with this truth, his first feeling is either that of dread or of a greed of gain. This drives him into wild exaggeration in worship, into frenzied convulsion of ceremonialism. But in Zarathushtra's teachings, which are best reflected in his Gathas, we have hardly any mention of the ritualism of worship. Conduct and its moral motives, such as Vohumano, Asha and Aramaiti, have received almost the sole attention in them.

The orthodox Persian form of worship in ancient Iran included animal sacrifices and offering of *haoma* to the *daevas*. That all this should be discountenanced by Zarathushtra not only shows his courage, but the strength of his realisation of the Supreme Being as Spirit. We are told that it has been mentioned by Plutarch: "Zarathushtra taught the Persians to sacrifice to Ahura Mazda 'vows and thanksgivings.'" The distance between faith in the efficacy of blood-stained magical rites and cultivation of moral and spiritual ideals as the true form of worship is immense. It is amazing to see how Zarathushtra was the first among men who crossed this distance with a certainty of realisation which imparted such a fervour of faith in his life and his words. The truth which filled his mind was not a thing borrowed from books or received from teachers. He did not come to it by following a prescribed path of tradition. It flashed upon him as an illumination of his entire life, almost like a communication to his personal self, and he proclaimed the utmost immediacy of his knowledge in these words:

"When I conceived of Thee, O Mazda, as the very First and the Last, as the most Adorable One, as the Father of Good Thought, as the Creator of Truth and Right, as the Lord Judge of our actions in life, then I made a place for Thee in my very eyes."—Yasna, 31–8. (Translation by D. J. Irani.)

It was the direct stirring of his soul which made him say:—

"Thus do I announce the Greatest of all. I weave my songs of praise for Him through Truth, helpful and beneficent to all that live. Let Ahura Mazda listen to them with His Holy Spirit, for the Good Mind instructed me to adore Him; by His Wisdom let Him teach me about what is best."—Yasna, 45–6.

The truth which is not reached through the analytical

process of reasoning, and does not depend for proof on some corroboration of outward facts, or the prevalent faith and practice of the people—the truth, which comes like an inspiration out of context with its surroundings, brings with it an assurance that it has been sent from a divine source of wisdom; that the individual who has received it is specially chosen and therefore has his responsibility as the messenger of God. Zarathushtra felt this sacredness of his mission and believed himself to be the direct medium of communication of Divine Truth.

So long as man deals with his God as the dispenser of benefits to the worshipper, who knows the secret of propitiating him, he tries to keep him for his own self or for the tribe to which he belongs. But directly the moral or spiritual nature of God is apprehended, this knowledge is thrown open to all humanity; and then the idea of God, which once gave unity only to a special people, transcends limitations of race and gathers together all human beings within one spiritual circle of union. Zarathushtra was the first prophet who emancipated religion from the exclusive narrowness of the tribal God, the God of a chosen people, and offered it to the universal man. This is a great fact in the history of religion. The Master said, when the enlightenment came to him:

"Verily I believe Thee, O Ahura Mazda, to be the Supreme Benevolent Providence, when Sraosha came to me with the Good Mind, when first I received and became wise with Thy words! And though the task be difficult, though woe may come to me, I shall proclaim to all mankind Thy message, which Thou declarest to be the best."—Yasna, 43-11.

He prays to Mazda:

"This I ask Thee, tell me truly, O Ahura, the religion that is best for all mankind—the religion, based on truth, which should prosper all that is mine, the religion which establishes our actions in order and justice by the Divine Songs of Perfect Piety, which has, for its intelligent desire of desires, the desire for Thee, O Mazda!"—Yasna, 44-10.

With the undoubted assurance and hope of one who has got a direct vision of Truth he speaks to the world:

"Hearken unto me, Ye, who come from far and near! Listen, for I shall speak forth now; ponder well over all things, weigh my words with care and clear thought. Never shall the false teacher destroy this world for a second time; for his tongue stands mute, his creed exposed."—Yasna, 45-1.

I think it can be said without doubt that such a high conception of religion, uttered in such a clear note of affirmation, with a sure conviction that it is a truth of the ultimate ideal of perfection which must be revealed to all humanity, even at the cost of martyrdom, is unique in the history of religion belonging to such a remote dawn of civilisation.

There was a time when along with other Aryan peoples the Persians also worshipped the elemental gods of nature, on whose favour they depended for the good things of life. But such favour was not to be won by any moral duty performed or by any service of love. In fact, it was the crude beginning of the scientific spirit trying to unlock the hidden sources of power in nature. But through it all there must have been some current of deeper desire which constantly contradicted the cult of power and indicated a world of inner good infinitely more precious than material gain. Its voice was not strong at first, nor was it heeded by the majority of the people ; but its influence, like the life within the seed, was silently working. Then comes the great teacher ; and in his life and mind the hidden fire of truth suddenly bursts out in a flame. The best in the people works for long obscure ages in hints and whispers till it finds its voice, which can never again be silenced. For that voice becomes the voice of mankind, no longer confined to a particular time or people. It works across intervals of silence and oblivion, depression and defeat, and comes out again and again with its conquering call. It is a call to the fighter—the fighter against untruth—against all that lures away man's spirit from its high mission of freedom into the meshes of materialism. And Zarathushtra's voice is still a living voice, not a mere matter of academic interest for historical scholars who deal with the dead facts of the past. It is not a voice which is only to guide a small community of men in the daily details of their life. For have we not seen that Zarathushtra was the first of all teachers who, in his religious teachings, sent his words to all human races across the distance of space and time ? He was not like a man who by some chance of friction had lighted a lamp, and knowing that it could not be shared by all, secured it with a miser's care for his own domestic use. But he was the watcher in the night, who stood on the lonely peak facing the East and broke out singing the poems of light to the sleeping world when the sun came out on the brim of the horizon. He declared that the sun of truth is for all, that its light is to unite the far and the near. Such a message always arouses the antagonism of those whose habits have become nocturnal, whose vested interest is in the darkness. And there was a bitter fight in the lifetime of the prophet between his followers and others who were addicted to the ceremonies that had tradition on their side and not truth.

We are told that "Zarathushtra was descended from a kingly family," and also that the first converts to his doctrines were of the ruling caste. But the priesthood, "the Kavis and the Karapans, often succeeded in bringing the rulers over to their side." So we find that, in this fight, the princes of the land divided themselves into two opposite parties, as we find in India in the Kurukshetra war. "With the princes have the Kavis and the Karapans united, in order to corrupt man by their evil deeds." Among the princes that stood against Zarathushtra, as his enemies, the mighty Bendva might be included, who is mentioned in Yasna, xlix, 1–2. From the context we may surmise that he stood on the side of the infidels. A family or a race of princely blood were probably the Grehma (Yasna, xxxii, 12–14). Regarding them it is said that they "having allied with the Kavis and the Karapans, have established their power in order to overpower the prophet and his partisans. In fact, the opposition between the pious and the impious, the believers and the unbelievers, seem very often to have led to open combat. The prophet prays to Ahura that he may grant victory to his own, when both the armies rush together in combat, whereby they can cause defeat among the wicked, and procure for them strife and trouble."

There is evidence in our Indian legends that in ancient

India also there have been fights between the representatives of the orthodox faith and the Kshatriyas, who, owing to their own special vocation, had a comparative freedom of mind about the religion of external observances. The proofs are strong enough to lead us to believe that the monotheistic religious movement had its origin and principal support in the kingly caste of those days, though a great number of them fought to oppose it.

I have discussed in another place the growth in ancient India of the moral and spiritual element in her religion which had accompanied the Indian Aryan people from the time of the Indo-Iranian age, showing how the struggle with its antagonistic force has continued all through the history of India. I have shown how the revolution which accompanied the teachings of Zarathushtra, breaking out into severe fights, had its close analogy in the religious revolution in India whose ideals are still preserved in the Bhagavadgita.

It is interesting to note that the growth of the same ideal in the same race in different geographical situations has produced results that, in spite of their unity, have some aspect of difference. The Iranian monotheism is more ethical, while the Indian is more metaphysical in its character. Such a difference in their respective spiritual developments was owing, no doubt, to the more active vigour of life in the old Persians and the contemplative quietude of mind in the Indians. This distinction in the latter arises in a great measure out of the climatic conditions of the country, the easy fertility of the soil and the great stretch of plains in Northern India affording no constant obstacles in physical nature to be daily overcome by man, while the climate of Persia is more bracing and the surface of the soil more rugged. The Zoroastrian ideal has accepted the challenge of the principle of evil and has enlisted itself in the fight on the side of Ahura Mazda, the great, the good, the wise. In India, although the ethical side is not absent, the emphasis has been more strongly laid on subjective realisation through a stoical suppression of desire, and the attainment of a perfect equanimity of mind by cultivating indifference to all causes of joy and sorrow. Here the idea, over which the minds of men brooded for ages, in an introspective intensity of silence, was that man as a spiritual being had to realise the truth by breaking through his sheath of self. All the desires and feelings that limit his being are keeping him shut in from the region of spiritual freedom.

In man the spirit of creation is waiting to find its ultimate release in an ineffable illumination of Truth. The aspiration of India is for attaining the infinite in the spirit of man. On the other hand, as I have said before, the ideal of Zoroastrian Persia is distinctly ethical. It sends its call to men to work together with the Eternal Spirit of Good in spreading and maintaining Kshatra, the Kingdom of Righteousness, against all attacks of evil. This ideal gives us our place as collaborators with God in distributing His blessings over the world.

" Clear is this all to the man of wisdom as to the man who carefully thinks ; he who upholds Truth with all the might of his power, he who upholds Truth the utmost in his word and deed, he, indeed, is thy most valued helper, O Mazda Ahura ! "—Yasna, 31-22.

It is, in fact, of supreme moment to us that the human world is in an incessant state of war between that which will save us and that which will drag us into the abyss of disaster. Our one hope lies in the fact that Ahura Mazda is on our side if we choose the right course. The law of warfare is severe in its character; it allows no compromise. "None of you," says Zarathushtra, "shall find the doctrine and precepts of the wicked; because thereby he will bring grief and death in his house and village, in his land and people! No, grip your sword and cut them down!"—Yasna, xxxi, 18.

Such a relentless attitude of fight reminds us of the Old Testament spirit. The active heroic aspect of this religion reflects the character of the people themselves, who later on spread their conquests far and wide and built up great empires by the might of their sword. They accepted this world in all seriousness. They had zest in life and confidence in their own strength. They belonged to the western half of Asia, and their great influence travelled through the neighbouring civilisation of India and towards the Western Continent. Their ideal was the ideal of the fighter. By the force of their will and deed of sacrifice they were to conquer *haurvatat*, welfare in this world, and *ameratat*, immortality in the other. This is the best ideal of the West, the great truth of fight. For Paradise has to be gained through conquest. That sacred task is for the heroes, who are to take the right side in the battle and the right weapons.

RABINDRANATH TAGORE.

THE DIVINE SONGS OF ZARATHUSHTRA

I

With bended knees, with hands outstretched, I pray to Thee, my Lord,
Invisible benevolent Spirit!
Vouchsafe to me in this hour of joy,
All righteousness of action, all wisdom of the Good Mind,
That I may thereby bring joy to the soul of creation.

II

He who, in the first beginning, thus thought: "Let the glorious heavens be clothed in light,"
He, by His supreme Understanding, created the principles of Truth and Right,
Enabling mortals thereby to maintain the Good Mind;
O Wise Lord, O ever-the-same Ahura, by Thy Holy Spirit make these realms to flourish!

III

The Supreme, the Best Being of all, the Source of Light for the world, art Thou, O Mazda!
As the Fountain of Light, as the World-Creator, Thou revealest Thyself, O most benevolent Mazda!
With Thy love, bless us with all things good, for all the days of a long life, O Mazda!

IV

Grant me, O Truth, the blessing which is the fruit of the Good Mind!
Grant me, O Piety, to me and to Vistaspa, our cherished desires!
And grant, O Mazda, my sovereign Lord, that reciting Thy holy words of revelation, I may make Thy felicitous Message heard!

V

Come Thou, Eternal Spirit of Life!
Come, through the Good Mind!
Come, with Thy gifts for Righteousness!
For his sublime and righteous words, give Thou to Zarathushtra and to us Thy gracious help, O Mazda,
Whereby we may overcome the evil of the wrong-doers.

VI

Ahura Mazda, and Spirit of Truth!
Grant These, my followers, such strength and spiritual power,
That with the help of the Benevolent Mind they may bring to the world restful joy and happiness,
Of which Thou, my Lord, art indeed the First Possessor!

VII

I shall take the soul to the House of Songs, with the help of the Good Mind!
Knowing the blissful rewards of Ahura Mazda for righteous deeds,
As long as I have power and strength, I shall teach all to seek for Truth and Right.

VIII

Through these divine songs,
For evermore shall I preserve Righteousness and the Good Mind for the people.
To enable me to apprise all, teach me, O Mazda,
In Thine own Spirit and in Thy words,
The principles of existence of this First Life.

IX

Unto Thee, O Lord, the Soul of Creation cried,—
"For whom didst Thou create me, and who so
fashioned me?
Feuds and fury, violence and the insolence of might,
have oppressed me;
None have I to protect me save Thee,
Command for me, then, the blessings of a settled,
peaceful life."

X

Mazda knows best what works have been wrought
by the followers of evil and by mortal men;
And He knows what shall be wrought by them for
ever hereafter.
The Lord Ahura is the discerning Judge;
To us let it be as He shall will.

XI

Thus we two, my soul and the soul of creation,
prayed with hands outstretched to the Lord Ahura,
Thus we two urged Mazda with entreaties,—
" Let not destruction overtake the right-living,
Let not the diligent good suffer at the hands of the evil."

XII

Thus spake Ahura Mazda :—
" The one, who alone has hearkened to my commands and is known to me, is Zarathushtra Spitama ;
For his Creator and for Truth, he wishes to announce my Holy Message ;
Wherefore I shall bestow on him the charm of speech."

XIII

When shall Truth, the Good Mind, and Holy Sovereignty, hasten to me, my Lord?
Do Thou assign them to me for the sake of the Great Dispensation!
And verily grant now to us, Thy devoted servants, Thine own gracious help for this Great Cause!

XIV

When shall I know, O Ahura, how Thou dost rule with Truth and Justice
Over those who oppress me and cast me in fear and doubt?
Aright for me, the Saviour-to-be, let the woven word of delight be given,
The word of beatific mystery, what the blessed End is to be!

XV

Tell me, my Lord,
The reward Thou shalt give by Thy Spirit and by Thy Fire,
The blessing Thou shalt assign, through Truth, to those fighting for Thy Cause,
The holy law meant for the enlightened.
Tell me about these all, in Thine own words and with Thine own lips,
That I may thereby cause all that are living to follow Thy Right Path.

XVI

O ye, who come to seek knowledge, now shall I proclaim to you the joyful message of the Wise Creator,
The hymns unto Ahura, and the prayer-offerings of the Good Mind,
The sublime Truth I see arising from these sacred flames,
And the glorious vision of the Heavenly Lights attainable through Truth sublime.

XVII

Hearken with your ears to these best counsels :
Gaze at these beams of fire and contemplate with your best judgment ;
Let each man choose his creed, with that freedom of choice which each must have at great events ;
O ye, awake to these my announcements !

XVIII

In the beginning, there were two Primal Spirits, Twins spontaneously active ;
These are the Good and the Evil, in thought, and in word, and in deed :
Between these two, let the wise choose aright ;
Be good, not base.

XIX

And when these Twin Spirits came together at first,
They established Life and Non-Life,
And so shall it be as long as the world shall last;
The worst existence shall be the lot of the followers of evil,
And the Good Mind shall be the reward of the followers of good.

XX

Of these Twin Spirits, the Evil One chose to do the worst;
While the bountiful Holy Spirit of Goodness,
Clothing itself with the massy heavens for a garment, chose the Truth;
And so will those who would fain please Ahura Mazda with righteous deeds, performed with faith in Truth.

XXI

Let him that knows tell him that would know, which of the two creeds is better,
The belief of the righteous, or of the liar?
Let not the unenlightened deceive you any more!
Be Thou to us, O Mazda Ahura, the bestower of Good Thought.

XXII

So may we be like those making the world progress towards perfection;
May the Lord and His Angels help us and guide our efforts through Truth;
For a thinking man is where Wisdom is at home.

XXIII

Then at last shalt Thou come, with Thy bountiful Spirit, O Mazda,
With Thy sovereign power, and with Thy Good Mind,
Which bringeth prosperity to the people of the world.
Perfect Truth shall teach to these people the Eternal Laws of Thy Wisdom,
The Wisdom which none can deceive.

XXIV

And when there cometh Divine Retribution for the Evil One,
Then at Thy command shall the Good Mind establish the Kingdom of Heaven, O Mazda,
For those who will deliver Untruth into the hands of Righteousness and Truth.

XXV

Then truly cometh the blow of destruction on Untruth,
And all those of good fame are garnered up in the Fair Abode,
The Fair Abode of the Good Mind, the Wise Lord, and of Truth!

XXVI

O ye mortals, mark these commandments—
The commandments which the Wise Lord has given, for Happiness and for Pain;
Long punishment for the evil-doer, and bliss for the follower of Truth,
The joy of Salvation for the Righteous ever afterwards!

XXVII

If through this Message ye realise the Eternal Truths,
and recognise the better life,
Then shall I come to you all, and help you in your
right selection between the Twin-Spirits,
And then, indeed, shall we all live our lives in
accordance with Truth and Right.

XXVIII

I pray to Thee, my Lord,
Give me the help of Truth, at a moment supremely
crucial,
Give me the help of Thy valiant captains, O Mazda !
Give me the help of the blessed Armaiti, the Angel of
loving Piety,
And give me that holy sovereign power, O Lord,
That I may for ever vanquish thereby the Evil Spirit
of Untruth.

XXIX

Teach me, my Lord, to discriminate what Thou, through
Right, hast appointed for me as the better portion ;
Teach me, my Lord, with the help of the Good Mind,
to know and to cherish my rights ;
And apprise me, O Mazda, of all things that are to be
and not to be.

XXX

When I conceived of Thee, O Mazda,
As the very First, and the Last,
As the Most Adorable One,
As the Father of Good Thought,
As the veritable Creator of Truth and Right,
As the Lord Judge of our actions in Life,
Then I made a place for Thee in my very eyes !

XXXI

Thus do I announce the Greatest of all!
I weave my songs of praise for Him through Truth—
helpful and beneficent to all that live.
Let Ahura Mazda hearken unto them with His Holy Spirit,
For the Good Mind instructed me to adore Him;
By His Wisdom let Him teach me what is best.

XXXII

Then I will ask Thee, O Mazda,
Of the events happening and the events to happen,
What requitals, in accord with their deeds, are appointed for the truthful righteous, and what for the lying sinners;
What shall be the consummation when they come to the last reckoning.

XXXIII

And this I ask Thee, O Ahura Mazda!
The truthful righteous striving to further the well-being
of his house, his province and his country,
How shall he be like unto Thee?
When shall he be worthy of Thee?
What actions of his shall most appeal to Thee?

XXXIV

Clear is all this to the man of wisdom, as to the man
who carefully thinks,
He who upholds Truth with all the might of his power,
He who upholds Truth to the utmost in his word and
deed,
He, indeed, is Thy most valued helper, O Mazda Ahura!

XXXV

To him, who is Thy true friend in spirit and in actions, O Mazda Ahura,
To him Thou shalt give Healthful Weal and Immortality;
To him Thou shalt give perpetual communion with Truth and the Kingdom of Heaven,
And to him Thou shalt give the sustaining strength of the Good Mind.

XXXVI

But whoso deceiveth the good and the righteous,
For him shall be the future long life of misery and darkness, woe and despair.
O ye men of evil lives! Your own deeds shall lead you to this dark existence.

XXXVII

Oh evil ones,
Ye are a seed of the evil mind,
Ye are a seed of arrogance and perversity!
And so are those that honour you!
Your evil deeds have long been known in the seven
regions of the earth.

XXXVIII

For ye liars confound the human mind, and make
men act their worst,
Make them speak as lovers of Untruth,
Rejected of the Good Mind,
Departing from the will of the Lord Mazda,
Divorced from Truth and Right.

XXXIX

Ah, the teacher of Evil!
The teacher of Evil destroys the Understanding;
He destroys the design of life,
Snatches away the only blessed and real wealth of the Good Mind!
With these words, proceeding from my very heart and spirit, I cry and complain to Thee, O Mazda, and to the Spirit of Truth.

XL

Listen, listen unto the Teller of Truth,
Listen unto him who thinks of Right and Truth,
Listen unto him, the enlightened and the knowing,
Who, standing before Thy holy Fire, O Mazda, with his powerful words and free tongue,
Reveals the Truth to the contending sides.

XLI

He who is most good to the righteous,
Be he a noble, or a peasant, or a dependent—
He who zealously cares for cattle and protects God's good creation,
He shall be hereafter in the beautiful realm of Truth and the Good Mind.

XLII

He who shows the righteous path of truth and happiness, both in this world and in the next, which is Thy abode, O Ahura,
Attains an end better than the good.
A generous helper, a noble citizen, a faithful follower worthy of Thee is he, O Mazda!

XLIII

He who abhors the light of the sun,
He who refuses to behold, with both his eyes, God's good creation,
He who makes offerings to the wicked,
He who makes the meadows waterless and the pastures desolate,
He who lets fly his weapon against the innocent,
An enemy of my faith, a destroyer of my principles, is he, O Mazda!

XLIV

And these evil-doers,
Who dwell in the abode of the worst mind,
Who yearn for ill-gotten gains,
Who wantonly destroy life,
Who obtaining a wish yet seethe in discontent
—These Kavis and Karpans—
Debarred of Thy Prophet's Message,
They shall not behold the beatific Vision of Truth.

XLV

O ye, men and women!
When the tainted cravings and selfish desires innermost in you are all rooted out,
When all the evil within you is suppressed for ever,
Then shall the Blessed Reward be yours for the Great Work!
And if ye fail, then, "Alas! Alas!" will be your ultimate cry.

XLVI

He who fights Evil, either by his thought or word,
Or with the might of his two hands,
He who instructs people to their good,
Makes a worthy offering of faith, in his love of Thee, O Ahura Mazda!

XLVII

With Thy Message shall I undo the work of the evil-doers.
No more shall the wicked Kavis and Karpans rule over the lives of the Righteous;
And the Angels of Healthful Weal and Deathless Immortality shall escort the good to the Abode of the Good Mind.

XLVIII

In times of doubt, O Mazda Ahura!
In times of stress and strife, Thou Best One!
When the vengeful harm of the wicked threatens us,
We shall recall all the best Thou hast taught us,
In the wide bright glow of the Altar-flame!

XLIX

Come hither to me, in Thine own Person, Ahura Mazda !
Come to my rites, Thou Best One !
Come with Thy Spirit of Truth and Thy Good Mind !
Let my message be listened to beyond the limits of the cultured ;
Let the precious offerings of humble prayers be manifest to all.

L

Do Thou make known to me the ultimate good, the final end,
Then shall I bring about the Consummation with the help of the Good Mind !
Accept, O Mazda, the loving homage of Thy devoted servants ;
Accept, O Truth, my hymn of praise for Thee ;
Grant, grant to us, Spirits of Deathless Weal and Immortality, your own two everlasting blessings.

LI

This precious reward of Thine, O Mazda,
Thou givest by way of the Good Mind—
Thou givest to the vigorous bodily life of him who works for and tends to Thy Creation,
Who furthers Thy beneficent plan by the toil of his understanding,
Guided verily by Thy Spirit of Truth.

LII

And with the blessings of these comrade spirits of Deathless Well-being and Immortality,
Let all advance to Thee, O Mazda!
Let all advance the Cause of Truth!
Let all advance to the Shining Abode of Wisdom, with a mind best-fitted for it!
Sure is the support of these Twain whose Spirits work together.

LIII

All the joys of life, which Thou holdest, O Mazda!
The joys that were, the joys that are, and the joys that shall be,
Thou dost apportion all in Thy Love for us.
O Wise Lord! through Thy sovereign authority let us advance to the desired beatitude,
With the help of the Good Mind, with the help of Truth!

LIV

Hearken unto me,
O most benevolent Ahura Mazda!
O ye Spirits of Devotion and Truth that bless our existence!
O Good Mind, and Dominion of Heaven!
Hearken unto me, be merciful to me, help me in all my actions!

LV

Arise, arise for me, O Ahura Mazda!
Through Thy most bounteous Spirit, purify me!
Through my good devotion, give me vigour and strength!
Through the guiding Spirit of Truth, give me courage and spiritual might!
And through the Good Mind, make me the Leader of the Good!

LVI

With Thy divine and helpful grace, O Mazda Ahura,
Make wide the vision of my mind;
Make manifest Thine everlasting attributes;
Make known the blessings of Thy Kingdom of Heaven and the joyous recompense of the Good Mind!
Angel of Love and Devotion, through Truth enlighten all with the right principles of Thy Faith!

LVII

To the Lord Mazda, as an offering,
Zarathushtra dedicates the life and vigour of his own body,
The choicest essence of his Good Thought;
To Truth with its principles he consecrates obedience, in word and deed, and all the might of his spiritual authority!

LVIII

What is Thy power? And what is Thy wealth, O Mazda?
How can my actions be likened unto Thine, my Lord?
Indeed thus: Through Righteousness and through a benevolent mind, by nourishing and succouring Thy poor, O Ahura!
We will declare this before all—both to the robber gangs and to the evil and poor-minded men.

LIX

Where are those helpers, O Mazda, enlightened of the Good Mind,
Who, even in times of woe,
Would stand by Thy treasured doctrines and spread wide the light of Thy Faith ?
None do I know other than Thee, O Truth, to protect and save us.

LX

Happiness be the lot of him who works for others' happiness.
May the Supreme Lord grant him the powers of health and strength !
For the struggle to uphold Truth, I beseech these very gifts from Thee, O Lord !
Mayst Thou, through Armaiti, the Angel of loving Piety, bless me with perfection and a life guided by the Good Mind !

LXI

Verily, I will regard Thee as the All-Powerful Benefactor, O Mazda !
For with Thy cherishing hand Thou offerest help both to the righteous as well as to the wicked.
Through the flaming splendour of Thy Fire, mighty through Truth,
The vigour of a good mind has come to me, O Mazda !

LXII

Verily, I believed Thee, O Ahura Mazda, to be the supreme benevolent Providence,
For I beheld Thee as the Primeval Cause of all creation.
For by Thy perfect Intelligence Thou shalt render just recompense for all actions, good to the good, evil to the evil, till the last day of creation.

LXIII

Verily, I believed Thee, O Mazda, to be the supreme benevolent Providence,
When Sraosha, with the Good Mind, came and asked me :—
" Who art thou ? " " Whose art thou ? " " How dost thou propose to enlighten the hearts of men in this country and answer their questionings ? "

LXIV

To him I replied : " Firstly, I am Zarathushtra.
A veritable enemy to the evil-doer, but a joy-giving powerful friend to the good, am I."
So long as I can praise Thee, and weave my songs for Thee, O Mazda !
So long shall I strive to enlighten and awaken all to the realisation of Thy absolute sovereignty.

LXV

Verily, I believed Thee, O Ahura Mazda, to be the supreme benevolent Providence,
When Sraosha, with the Good Mind, came and asked me,
" What gift wouldst thou love to obtain ? "
Standing at Thy Fire in humble prayer, I replied :
" So far as it is in my power, I shall cherish the gift of Righteousness."

LXVI

Verily, I believed Thee, O Ahura Mazda, to be the supreme benevolent Providence,
When Sraosha came to me with the Good Mind,
When first I received and became wise with Thy words !
And though the task be difficult, though woe may come to me,
I shall proclaim to all mankind Thy Message, which Thou declarest to be the best.

LXVII

Verily, I believed Thee, O Ahura Mazda, to be the supreme benevolent Providence,
When Sraosha came to me with the Good Mind, and told me assuringly,
That a contented mind is the best possession ;
Let not a leader try to please and propitiate evil-doers,
For they treat the righteous as harmful enemies.

LXVIII

O Ahura Mazda, thus prays Zarathushtra and all holy men who have chosen as their guide Thy most benevolent Spirit :—
" May Righteousness, strong with vital vigour, become incarnate in the faithful !
In Thy sun-lit realms, may Armaiti, the Angel of Love and Devotion, reside !
Through the Good Mind, may righteous recompense be granted to all in accordance with their deeds ! "

LXIX

This I ask Thee, tell me truly, O Ahura!
What is the source of the Best Existence?
How do those who seek for it get the blessed recompense?
Verily a benevolent bountiful Providence,
A Guardian warding off ruin from all,
A genuine Friend of the people, art Thou, O Mazda!

LXX

This I ask Thee, tell me truly, O Mazda!
Who so balanced the earth and the heavens, and keeps them from falling away?
Who created the waters and the plants?
Who yoked swiftness to the winds and motion to the clouds?
Who save Thyself is the Creator of the Good Mind, O Mazda?

LXXI

This I ask Thee, tell me truly, O Ahura!
What great artist created light and darkness?
What artisan produced the calm of restful sleep and the zeal of active life?
Who made the dawn, the moon, and the night,
That, like monitors, call enlightened men to their duties?

LXXII

This I ask Thee, tell me truly, O Ahura!
What are Thy maxims for my meditation, O Mazda?
Which are the Divine Hymns, inspired by the Good Mind, I had asked for?
What songs of Truth will bring me the allegiance of people?
How shall my soul partake of the Good that is ever on the increase?

LXXIII

This I ask Thee, tell me truly, O Ahura,
The religion that is the best for all mankind,—
The religion, based on Truth, which should prosper all that is mine,
The religion which establishes our actions in order and justice by the Divine Songs of perfect Piety,
Which has for its intelligent desire of desires, the Desire for Thee, O Mazda!

LXXIV

This I ask Thee, tell me truly, O Ahura!
How shall I drive away the Spirit of Untruth, the Lie-demon from amongst us,
To those beneath, to the unfaithful and the disobedient,
Who strive not to be the companions of Truth,
Who care not to listen to the counsels of the Good Mind?

LXXV

This I ask Thee, tell me truly, O Ahura!
How shall I deliver the Lie into the hands of Truth?
When shall I smite her by the holy hymns of Thy True Faith?
How shall I destroy the evil liars before they attain their object?

LXXVI

This I ask Thee, tell me truly, O Ahura!
How can my yearning love attract Thee to me?
How can I attain to Thy Perfection, and make my voice effectual?
Through these Divine songs, which receive their guiding light from Truth,
May all receive the two gifts of Well-being and Immortality during my protecting leadership!

LXXVII

This I ask Thee, tell me truly, O Ahura!
He who will not give due recompense to the one who well earns it,
Even unto the truthful man who fulfils his word and work,
What penalty should he pay first here?
For verily, I know well what he will get at the last hereafter.

LXXVIII

Hearken unto me,
O ye, who come from near and from far!
Listen! Listen unto me, for I shall speak forth now,
Ponder well over all things,
Weigh my words with care and clear thought;
Never shall the False Teacher destroy this world for a second time,
For his tongue stands mute, his creed stands exposed.

LXXIX

I shall tell you now of the Twin Spirits, at the first
  beginning of Creation ;
The Holier of the two thus spake to the Evil One :—
" Neither our thoughts, nor our teachings,
Neither our intelligence, nor our beliefs,
Neither our words, nor our deeds,
Neither our selves, nor our souls, ever agree."

LXXX

I shall tell you now what is best in this life,
It is to act in consonance with the Spirit of Truth,
  the holy Asha,
As Mazda Ahura knows, who created him—
Ahura Mazda, the father of the toiling Good Mind,
Ahura Mazda, the father of Armaiti, of good action
  and zeal,
Ahura Mazda, the All-Seeing, whom none can deceive !

LXXXI

I shall tell you now what the Most Holy declared to me,
As the word that is best for mortals to hear and obey :—
" To all who shall render obedience to Me, I shall come ;
I shall come unto them with the blessings of Welfare and Immortality, for the actions of their Good Spirit."
Thus spake Ahura Mazda.

LXXXII

On Thy behalf, then, shall I speak forth, O Mazda !
As one that knows to those who fain would know :—
" Evil is the portion of the wicked,
But the wished-for beatitude, the Best Mental State, is for the man who maintains for himself the Law of Truth."
To announce this message to the wise is the joy of Thy Messenger.

LXXXIII

Those who are living, those who have been, and those
who are yet to be,
Shall attain one of the two awards which He ordains!
In Immortality shall the soul of the Righteous be
ever in Joy,
But in torment the soul of the Liar shall surely be.
And these Laws hath Ahura Mazda ordained through
His sovereign authority.

LXXXIV

With my songs of praise, with my self-humbling
worship, I wish to serve my Lord!
For now, indeed, I see Him with my own eyes, the
Lord of the Good Spirit, the Lord of the good
word and deed.
I know Him through Truth, who is Ahura Mazda!
Verily, I shall render Him my homage in the House
of Songs.

LXXXV

My Lord, when shall the day dawn for winning the world to the cause of Truth?
When shall the wise Spiritual Guides come with the sublime teachings of Thy Chosen Saviour?
To the help of whom shall they come with the Good Mind?
As for me, I have chosen Thee as my instructor, Ahura Mazda.

LXXXVI

When are the men of wisdom coming, O Mazda?
When shall they remove the filthy evil of intoxication,
The fell evil of drink, by which the lying Karpans and the wicked lords of the lands
Make desolate the world?

LXXXVII

When, O Mazda, shall Piety come with Truth in our lands ?
When shall happy home-life, rich with heavy pastures, come to us through good government ?
Who shall bring peace to us from cruel and wicked men ?
To whom shall the wisdom of the Good Mind come, O Mazda !

LXXXVIII

Tell me, O Ahura, for Thou art the All-Knowing—
Shall the righteous overcome the evil, godless foe, when the great crisis overtakes us ?
For that were indeed a blessed glorious event for the world's regeneration.

LXXXIX

Yoke, yoke Thine ardent steeds, O Ahura Mazda!
Gain the passes to the Land of Thy Worship!
Yoke Thy mighty ones and come unto me with Thy Spirit of Truth and Thy Good Mind,
Come unto me, O hasten unto my help, O Mazda!

XC

When, with the Divine help of Truth, men shall conquer the Lie,
When deceptions and untruths—for long decried—of false gods and baser men stand bare in their ugly nakedness,
Then Thy worship will blossom in its fullness, bearing the fruit of its rich blessings!

XCI

Verily, the Right of the truthful man shall vanquish at last the Wrong of the wicked.
Standing at the Bridge of Judgment,
The Evil Soul shall behold open the path of the righteous ;
He strives to reach it, but his own deeds prove to be his fetters ;
Trembling and moaning, he finds that he fails.

XCII

He who applies well his mind, and sifts things better from things worse,
He who applies well his mind to deepen his insight into Faith,
His wish is in harmony with his cherished and chosen ideals ;
His happy end, at the last, is indeed within Thy Understanding, O Mazda !

XCIII

Whoever, man or woman, shall do what Thou, O Ahura Mazda, knowest to be the Best in Life,
Whoever shall do right for the sake of Right,
Whoever, in authority, shall govern only by the aid of the Good Mind,
To all these shall I teach the songs of Thy Praise;
Forth shall I lead them all, over the Bridge of Judgment.

XCIV

O Frashoshtra, of the clan of Hvogva,
Go thou thither, with these faithful helpers, whom we both have chosen for the world's salvation,
Thither, where the gentle Armaiti with her active mind, goeth hand in hand with Truth,
Thither, where the Good Mind holds the reins of dominion,
Thither, where the Lord Mazda Himself abides in beatific Majesty in the Shining Abode of Desire.

XCV

O Maidio-Maha, of the Spitama family,
Whoso, after becoming learned and wise,
After gaining insight into Faith,
Out of his own love for mankind strives to do good unto all
Through the fruitful deeds of a better life,
And announces to them the laws of Truth and Right ordained by Mazda—
That man, so well offering his life's work, is an ally of the Great Cause !

XCVI

Jamaspa Hvogva, the lord of wealth and power, the follower of Truth,
Doth choose for himself the wisdom of Thy Faith, my Lord,
And so choosing attains to this royal heritage—
The Kingdom of the Good Mind.
Grant me, my Lord, that I may so teach the people
Ever to look for their shelter and protection in Thee, O Ahura !

XCVII

O Pouruchista, scion of the clans of Haechataspa and Spitama!
Youngest of the daughters of Zarathushtra!
The Lord Mazda has ordained for thee, as thy protecting lord,
Jamaspa, who is the constant ally of the Good Mind, the strenuous supporter of Truth and Right;
Take counsel with thine own understanding;
With devotion act well as thy wisdom may direct!

XCVIII

Pouruchista: "Verily, loving I shall vie with him in love.
Faithful to my father and to my husband,
Faithful to the peasants as to the nobles,
Faithful as a righteous woman should be to the righteous,
Mine shall be the glorious heritage—
The Light of the Good Mind!
May Ahura Mazda grant me this blessing that endureth for all time!"

XCIX

These words do I address to you, maidens marrying,
These counsels do I give to you, bridegrooms;
Pay heed to my words and lay them to heart:
Learn from the righteous the precepts of the Good Religion;
Let both strive to lead the life of the Good Mind;
With upright hearts love and cherish each other;
Then surely a happy home-life shall be yours!

C

And these are real facts, O ye men and women!
No happiness can be yours, if the Lie-demon drives the chariot of your lives;
Cast off from your selves all evil bonds that may chain you to Untruth;
Happiness linked with dishonour, happiness that harms others, is poison for the seeker.
The evil-faithless, who brings ruin to the righteous here, destroys for himself his spiritual life hereafter.

CI

The man of devotion is beneficent to all.
He is beneficent, because of his hallowed wisdom,
Because of his realisation of Truth,
Because of the goodness in his thoughts, in his words
    in his actions.
Unto him the Lord Ahura shall grant the Kingdom
    of the Good Mind !
And verily this good blessing I too am longing for !

CII

Then let them pay homage to the Lord Ahura !
Let them sing His Praise, and render worship,
Complete with the goodness of their thoughts, their
    words and their deeds.
May King Vistaspa, Frashoshtra, and the followers of
    Zarathushtra Spitama
Teach all to keep to the established straight paths of
    the Religion,
Which Ahura Mazda has ordained for the Princely
    Prophet and the future Spiritual Guides.

CIII

O all ye, working with one will,
Let Truth, Good Thought and Devotion,
Through which ye progress to the perfection of the bountiful Armaiti,
Bring to you the wished-for ultimate Happiness!
O Mazda Ahura! Yearning for the Joy that proceeds from Thee, our reverent homage we offer unto Thee!

CIV

Ah, the Abode of Songs!
The Lord, Ahura Mazda, was the First in the blessed Abode of Songs.
It is the Blessed Reward designated by me, Zarathushtra, for the supporters of the Great Cause!
All ye who hearken! It shall still be bestowed upon you,
If the Good Mind leads you,
If Truth guides your path!

CV

O ye who wish to be allied to the Good Mind, to be friends with Truth,
O ye who desire to sustain the Holy Cause,
Down with all anger and violence;
Away with all ill-will and strife!
Such benevolent men, O Mazda, I shall verily take to the House of Songs.

CVI

Tell me, O Mazda, how they should act and work,
Who love this joy-giving world with its wealth of heavy pastures?
(Answer:) "Living upright lives under the recurring splendours of the Sun,
Living in ordered settlements in harmony with the law of Truth,
These men shall reap the Blessed Reward!"

CVII

Let those who know well how to rule well, and not the evil-rulers, rule us !
Let them rule us with wisdom—rule us with good skill, O Piety !
O Thou Best One, make man perfect, and bless with a hallowed blessing his future life ;
Let man be active, zealously caring for his land and his cattle, for surely they nourish him.

CVIII

Where is the righteous ruler, to befriend the zealous and the diligent ?
Where do mercy and pardon lie ?
When shall Truth come into its own ?
Where is the bountiful Armaiti with her alert and active mind ?
Whence shall the Good Mind approach us ?
And where, O Mazda, where indeed is Thy Dominion and Sovereign Power ?

CIX

The daily toiler doth ask these questions,
That receiving guidance from Truth he may work for the world's welfare;
Ever wise in his devotion,
Ever upright in his actions,
He acknowledges the Spiritual Chief appointed for the well-being of all creation.

CX

A righteous government is of all things the most to be wished for,
Bearing the greatest blessings and good fortune to people,
Guided by the Law of Truth, worked with all wisdom and zeal,
It blossoms indeed into the Best of Rule, a Kingdom of Heaven!
To effect this for us, I will work now and ever.

CXI

When I beseech Thee for Grace and Knowledge, O Mazda!
Thy Spirit of Truth tells me what is within Thy Divine Wisdom,
Tells me ever to choose and to act aright,
That thereby the truths of Thy Holy Faith
May vividly be brought into light.

CXII

He who lifts his voice in the songs of Thy praise,
He who, impelled by Truth, kneels in all humility in Thy worship, O Lord!
He who directs his speech in the right path of wisdom,
A true friend of Zarathushtra is he!
Inspired by Thy Good Mind, verily he may announce my ordinance!

CXIII

All these indeed gather unto Thee, O Mazda,
Ever guarded by Thy blessings and Thy might,
Whose actions accord with Truth,
Whose words proceed from the Good Mind,
Whose First Teacher and Inspirer art Thou, O Mazda !

CXIV

At the last turning of life,
To the faithful, making the right choice, distributing
goodness among all,
Doth Ahura Mazda, the Lord Judge, in His Sovereign
Power,
Bestow an end better than the good.
But to him who hath no portion of good,
He giveth an end worse than the evil,
At the last turning of life !

CXV

The highest aspirations of Spitama Zarathushtra attain
fruition, my Lord,
When Thou dost grant him, for his perfect Righteousness,
The Existence Beautiful enduring for all times ;
When the unbelievers at last turn to him,
Eager to learn the Good Words and principles of Thy
Holy Faith !

CXVI

Singing the holy hymns of Thy Praise, my Lord,
Singing in the fullness of my heart,
With hands outstretched, I shall encompass Thee, O
Mazda !
Kneeling in humble prayer, with Truth and the Good
Mind by my side,
I shall verily reach Thy Presence, O Mazda !

CXVII

The good deeds that we do, and those we shall do
hereafter,
The good things that shine bright and look precious
to the eye,
The sun, the stars, the beautiful dawn—the herald
of the day,—
They all, in truth, sing Thy praise, O Mazda Ahura!

CXVIII

With these Divine Songs I shall come to meet Thee,
my Lord!
I shall come, in the company of Truth, aided by the
deeds of the Good Mind;
Seeking earnestly the reward of the beneficent, and
receiving it,
I shall be the Master of my own Destiny.

CXIX

The Poet of Thy Praise, I call myself, O Mazda!
And so shall I remain, O Truth, as long as my strength and power lasts.
Let the World-Creator help me through the Good Mind;
Through His Infinite Grace let that be done which shall best promote His Great Cause!

CXX

With Truth moving my heart,
With Best Thought inspiring my mind,
With all the might of spiritual force within me,
I kneel in homage to Thee, my Master, with the songs of Thy loving praise ever on my lips!
And even at the last, when I shall stand at Thy Gate as a suppliant,
I shall hear distinct the sweet echo of my prayers from Thy Abode of Songs.

NOTES

For the better appreciation of the writings of Zarathushtra it is worth while noting shortly the elements of his theology.

Zarathushtra was a complete monotheist. He further recognises that the Supreme Being, the Universal Soul, was and is the source of all perfect attributes. Six of such divine attributes he refers to in his writings. They are as follows :—

1. The Spirit of the Good Mind (Vohu Mano).

The Wise Lord is the fountain source of the Perfect Good Mind. It is placed first; for the Good Mind, or Good Thought, is the foundation on which the edifice of all goodness in words and in actions is based. Knowledge and Wisdom, the progressive fruits of the Good Mind, are included in its connotation.

2. The Spirit of Truth and Right (Asha).

Zarathushtra was among the earliest of mankind, if not the very first, to state that the Spirit of Truth was part of the very essence of the Supreme Being. Righteousness in thought, word, and deed being a phase of Truth, Asha includes them all within its meaning. From the principles of Truth and Right proceed the harmony of Universal Law and Order, and hence the term Asha is also often used to mean the Holy and Immutable Laws of the Universe.

3. The Spirit of Holy Sovereignty (Khashtra).

Ahura Mazda is the Supreme Sovereign Lord, and the term " Khashtra " refers to His Spiritual Sovereignty as well as to His Dominion of Heaven. Just as men can have the gifts of the Good Mind and Righteousness for themselves, so can they establish by means thereof a Kingdom of Heaven even on this earth, if they would only strive to do so.

4. The Spirit of Benevolent Devotion and Love (Spenṭa Armaiti).

It is described as of the active and zealous mind. Working diligently for the welfare of mankind, the motive force being its love for mankind, it is known as the "Bountiful Armaiti." A peasant toiling arduously on his native soil, rearing up his family in love, caring for his flock and lands, is more blest by the Spirit of Bountiful Armaiti than a recluse who has renounced the world and lives on alms. Hence loving devotion, diligence, and benevolence are not only commendable attributes, but become part of a religious duty.

5. The Spirit of Perfection and Healthful Well-being (Haurvatat).

6. The Spirit of Immortality (Ameratat).

These are said to be the Twin Spirits, or the Twin Blessings, which Providence awards to the man who yearns for and strives to possess the attributes of the

Almighty. As Zarathushtra says, in several places, a man or woman who is inspired by the Good Mind, whose actions are guided by Truth, who works lovingly and diligently for the welfare of God's Creation, who strives in his or her own humble way to make the world progress towards perfection, will certainly be blessed by Providence with the Twin Blessings of a Perfected and Happy Life here, and Immortality ever afterwards, in the Fair Abode of the Great Father.

Printed in the USA
CPSIA information can be obtained
at www.ICGtesting.com
LVHW082308251123
764922LV00007B/613